A TASTE OF THE KNIFE

by
Marnie Walsh

Ahsahta Press

Boise State University
Boise, Idaho

Some of these poems have appeared in:

Dacotah Territory, *Scree*, and *South Dakota Review*;

From the Belly of the Shark, edited by Walter Lowenfels (New York: Vintage Books, 1973); and

Voices from Wah'Kon-Tah, edited by Robert K. Dodge and Joseph P. McCullough (New York: International Publishers, 1974).

Editor for Ahsahta Press: Tom Trusky

Third Printing, February 1982

ISBN 0-916272-03-6

Library of Congress Catalog Card Number:
76-15877

Contents

Introduction *by John Milton*   iii

Vickie Loans-Arrow
   Fort Yates, No. Dak., 1970   1
Vickie Loans-Arrow
   1971   4
Vickie Loans-Arrow
   1972   6
Vickie Loans-Arrow
   1973   9
Herman Two-Lance
   Pine Ridge, So. Dak.   12
Angelina Runs-Against
   Pine Ridge, So. Dak.   14
Celia Coyote-Running
   Pine Ridge, So. Dak.   15
Thomas Holy-Flute   16
John Knew-The-Crow
   1880   17
Emmet Kills-Warrior
   Turtle Mountain Reservation   18
Seth Dismounts Thrice
   Rapid City, So. Dak., 1967   20
Charlie Two-Head
   White Shield, No. Dak., 1968   22
Bessie Dreaming Bear
   Rosebud, So. Dak., 1960   24
Lila Good-Weasel
   Standing Rock, No. Dak.   25
Thomas Iron-Eyes
   Born *circa* 1840.
   Died 1919, Rosebud Agency, S.D.   26
Last Summer It So Happened   29
Why I Choose to Live in the Desert   30
The Journey   31
Spirit Lake, Minnesota   32
June the Twenty-Second   33
New Year's Eve   34
Fishing on Lake Metigoshe   36
It Was The Season   37

The Red Fox   38
Poets/Poems   39
Poets/Poems   40
Poets/Poems   41
Dacotah Winter   42
A Successful Retirement   43
To Billie Jean: Streetwalker
     Who At One Time Was A Rockette   44

Introduction

As an outdoorswoman, an observer of hunters, Indians, creatures of nature, and the things of earth, Marnie Walsh seems to have been most impressed by the grimness of life. The sordid and the brutal, in both man and nature, enter her poems with more force and more power than do the lyrical elements of a very few of her poems. Most of these poems, especially in their observations of Indians, are character sketches with a persistent similarity. Their strength derives from accumulated evidence, from repetition which is much like the pounding of a drum. One beat is hardly distinguishable from another, but this sameness is an important part of her observations and implied interpretations. Especially in the sketches of Indians, where it is impossible to let the futility and the monotony of reservation life pass by unnoticed, the regularity of theme and technique operates like a *wacipi* drum, pounding its way into the reader's sensibilities.

In the individual poems, however, sensibility is not as important as the elementary description, the simple details of everyday life. Walsh is a keen observer, even though she may not like what she sees. In the character sketches she tries hard to enter the consciousness of each character, to pick up the language of the person she is writing about, and to say what is happening without her own editorializing. One way of doing this, of course is by juxtaposition:

> old bull-toes
> put his mark
> on our hands at the door

is immediately followed by an implied but striking contrast,

> white mens music
> up on the stage

and from these two facts, briefly mentioned, we are able to see a great deal about the tragic encounter of two cultures. In another juxtaposition, college life for a young woman gives way to drunkenness and pregnancy the moment she returns to the reservation.

Little is left to the imagination. Occasional images of discovery or beauty (a few of which almost become symbolic) are subordinated to realistic detail. To support the reality, especially in the Indian sketches, language remains on a rather primitive level. The Vickie pieces seem to come from a teen-ager, relatively illiterate and naive, exposed to constant drinking and fighting which are described in non-literary language, i.e., the language of Vickie. Walsh is trying to produce stark reality, to be literal rather than literary. The commonplace overshadows the unusual. There are no surprises. Rarely does anything humorous or "soft" interfere with the sordid elements of reality or offer relief from them. The poems, then, are like a protest against the conditions in which Indians live, both off and on the reservation, and their chief ingredient is the stating of the conditions.

There is, of course, method in this "madness." Ultimately, in the long Thomas poem, the traditional Indian way of life is formally contrasted with the present conditions under which he suffers. "What was" and "what is" are two entirely different things, and suddenly from the series of Indian poems comes a loud lament, a cry of sadness as well as anger, and the poems become a narrative centering on the plight of the Northern Plains Indian whom Walsh seems to know well from long association.

The bizarre, the grim, the literal reality continue into the non-Indian poems, but imagery and suggestiveness become more important as propaganda drops away and the poet and her poetry—as well as nature—become the subjects. A kind of sadness remains, as in "The Journey," but the sadness is driven deeper, as in "Spirit Lake, Minnesota," no longer a question of social criticism but of the very condition of nature and therefore of all life. This sadness is quite different from the grimness of the Indian poems or from "Last Summer It So Happened." It is contemplative, philosophical. The close relationship between the natural world and the human world ("June the Twenty-Second") lends a subtle dignity to both; it also provides images which have both feeling and a strong visual quality.

Marnie Walsh is a regionalist in the good sense of that term, examining her own land, her own neighbors, her own climate, her own familiar objects to see what they have in store for her and for those of us who read the poems. To "cast in ever wider circles / while the wind tricks my senses" is, among other things, to wander (as Marnie does) and let outside influences play upon the natural rootedness. But the focus of the perspective thus achieved is still on the nests of her own field, both literally and metaphorically.

Poems are true, in spite of Marnie's line which says that "The truthful man / makes a wretched poet." But they are true in at least two ways. One is suggested by the title of this book, *A Taste of the Knife*, which refers to a ceremony in which the messenger's truthfulness is tested by placing a knife in his mouth. If he cuts his tongue while speaking, he lies; if not, he speaks the truth. Most of the poems in this book speak that kind of truth, a literal and hard truth. The others are the "lies" that begin to "leave the taste of music / in our mouths." These are more suggestive, more lyrical, more literary. But still true. Whether Marnie Walsh is speaking harshly and literally about human conditions, or gently and metaphorically about poems, love, and nature, she speaks the truth.

John Milton
University of South Dakota
Vermillion

iv

Vickie Loans-Arrow
Fort Yates, No. Dak., 1970

1
i went to the dance
tommy little dog
ask me
i wait by the road
seen the red go
in the water   in the lake
then yellow spiderwebs
climb up the sky
one star watching
it get dark
tommys pickup come down the hill
i get in
saturday night is whisky
night
we drink   i forget
the red sun in the water

2
i hear
the agency hall
banging   shouting   stomping
i ready to dance
old bull-toes
put his mark
on our hands at the door
white mens music
up on the stage
christmas lights all around
one time i was the angel
up there
mama made me pretty wings
tommy was a shepherd
charlie two-head
baby jesus
he died after
i forget why

3
well
them white mens music
just what we like
for dancing
the floor go rockarock
i got on my red dress
my beads
tommy wear his sateen shirt
purple pink
we go round and round
push push
saturday night   whisky night

4
some old squaws
on benches next the wall
watch us
outside the old men
mostly drunk
spit on ground
drink   tell jokes
aunt nettie drunk
in her plymouth
on back seat
aunt nettie come back
to reservation
been to college
right away cecil dog-heart
give her baby
when she drunk
saturday nights
all the men get on her

5
we all drink vodka
at my cousins truck
everybody happy
everybody feeling good
lights all dusty
i got dusty eyes
so i not see right
joshua get mad

nobody care but tommy
they fight   fall down
joshua get a thing
out of truck
hit tommy on head
too much
it get all quiet
we go away

6
next day aunt nettie
say he dead
we dig potatoes a little
mama ask me
how i come home
if tommy dead
i say i forget
but i dont forget
when i seen the sun
all red
go in the water

Vickie Loans-Arrow
1971

1
when my aunt nettie was a kid
she stole real good
from out the stores
beads rings   easy things
stole more hard stuff later
the police catch her sometimes
but she so little
with soft eyes
they dont do nothing to her

2
but her papa beat her bad
to teach her good
and put her in catholic school
her mama cried at that
but nettie learnt everything
so easy that they say
she must come to college
and she did for a while

3
my aunt nettie was real pretty
when little and when she come home
she got a baby after a time
but give it away
then it seem she dont feel
like doing nothing
dont feel like stealing
just fools around
gets drunk
and screwed

4
sometimes she like to tell me
what all she done in college
she dont tell though
why she come home
nathan say she stole money

and got thrown out
i remember one time special
she told me some poetry
she liked   told it soft
about love and some lady in a tower
by a lake

5
when aunt nettie got too drunk
she told poetry
and oh she knowed it good
but all the people laughed
and she took to crying a lot
wouldnt eat
just drank whisky all the time
dont wear nice clothes
dont go to dances
got skinny and littler
till wasnt much left of her
no mama to care and no papa to beat her
they dead and her alone

6
yesterday they find her
all crazy
screaming and naked
she say she lost
and cant find her tower
by the lake
some people take her away
but not her poetry
i stole it
and she wont miss it   where she went

Vickie Loans-Arrow
1972

1
this morning
me and my cousin
charlene lost-nation
are in to bobby simons bar
and charlene say
i tired of living
there aint nothing in it
and bobby simon
behind the bar
goes ha ha ha
when she fall off
the stool
im laughing too
she so drunk
she funny

2
i get her up
then she say
there aint nothing in it
to them old white farmers
drinking their beer
and talking crops
they dont listen
dont even look at her
and bobby simon say
i see your mama out front
so we go out
and the sun so yellow
burn my eyes
and make charlenes mama
shiver like shes made
out of water
but it only the wind
all gold color
moving everything in waves

3
she say goddam you
charlene them kids of yours
come over and i got to
take them in
while you drunk all the time
i aint going to do it
no more
it too damn hot
i watch her shoes all torn
and wrinkly
and her fat legs
floating on the yellow wind
then charlene say
there aint nothing in it
it all plain shit
and we go back in the bar

4
we drink and she pulls
her face up tight
tells me it dont pay to think
theres something to it
cause there aint
and says wont nobody
never believe her
what she says
i just laugh
she so drunk
she funny

5
well me and bobby simon
drink some more
i seen charlene
when she gone to the can
she dont come back
pretty soon bobby simon
say i better check her out
so i go to see
i find her all right
sitting in a corner
theres blood on her mouth

and her chin
and down her dress

6
she looks at me
and i see the knife
sticking out between her teeth
and remember what that means
and i know shed like to die
but cant
so she killed her tongue
instead
i leave her there
i go out the door
and down the street
and the yellow wind
make me shiver and sweat
because now i believe her
but wont never say so

Vickie Loans-Arrow
1973

1
my brother nathan
comes home on leave
from the war on the bus
and we all there to meet him
snow is every place
deep and white
he picks it up in his hands
his eyes dont stop looking at it

2
my brothers friends is there too
george little elk and cousin wayne
who got a new car
from getting his leg shot off
where nathan been
my brother look quiet
when he seen how george
got bad nerves
that make him shake all over
and laugh like he cant close
his mouth no more

3
we all go home
and mama cooks lots to eat
it start to get dark over the snow
nathan go out and watch
he dont make no shadow
i think a shadow on snow
aint good to see anyway
then him and his friends
sit around and drink
say hey lets go to town
they pretty drunk and my brother
fall down in the snow
laughing and white all over
like somebodys ghost

4

he tell us all next morning
he run into his old girl friend
and she take him home
he dont know what happen
to wayne and george
there aint no girls want
no cripples or crazies
so say uncle morris
and nathan get terrible mad
throw his coffee at morris
and hollers goddam whores
goddam bitches
goddam world

5

then my brother run away
out the door in the snow
i follow him and see
he make just a little shadow
even in daytime
and it slides over the snow
like some old owl
he go over the hill to the road
and he the one find the car
that belong to cousin wayne
nathan seen it sticking up
out of the ditch
finds george some ways off
where he drug his self
cousin waynes head stuck half
through the windshield
not shaking no more

6

after that nathan dont talk much
no more and dont go nowhere
just sits to home drunk
then it time he go again
and we all take him to the bus
early in the morning dark
with some pink to the east
well the bus goes with nathan in it

my brother dont look back
dont look out the window
at the shadow running
in the snow beside it.

Herman Two-Lance
Pine Ridge, So. Dak.

1
mama got a job
in the moccasin factory
for the blue wing company
they get big boxes
cowhides all cut out
ready to sew
chauncey hollow horn
drive the trick
what brings them
from rapid city
mama sew the pieces
on a machine
other ladies sew too
they all the time laughing
telling gossip

2
in the blue wing factory
they got a coffee
machine
they got a machine makes it
warm inside in winter
cool in summer
got a machine
to sew on beads
when me and grandpa
go past where mama work
he make shaming noises
in his mouth

3
all day he just sit
in the yard
dont look at nothing
but the prairie
mama bring him tobacco
buy him warm coat
he dont wear it

cook him beans out of cans
his favorite
she get good money
from the blue wing company

4
one day she bring me
moccasins from there
grandpa hit her
she laugh and say
old man got old bones
is good for nothing
grandpa go outside
look out on the prairie
the wind blow his white hair
he sings sad old words
i dont know
what they mean
but i want to tell him
it dont matter
all of us
is good for nothing
but dont know how
so i cant

Angelina Runs-Against
Pine Ridge, So. Dak.

i got wine
a whole bottle
and i just set here
in the weeds
by the depot
and drink my wine
its too early
for them soldiers
and their fuckin
dollars
so i drink my wine
and wave at the trains
but nobody ever waves back

i never got money enough
for a ticket home
only for wine

Celia Coyote-Running
Pine Ridge, So. Dak.

winter nights on the reservation
grandma dishes up stew and stories
about the good times
when the war was on
and the white men built the place
to fly their planes from
about the good times
when she was fourteen like me
well she says the soldiers
come from all over with money
for whisky and girls
and having a red skin
made no difference atall
when having fun in the bushes
in halley park in town

she says when she was fourteen and pretty
she had such good times
everybody drunk and dancing in the bars
then she gets up from the table
to show how it was
she says them soldiers was so horny
theyd of laid her on the floor right there
every night grandma and her sister
name of shirley got drunk
got laid got paid so many dollars
her pocketbook was overfull
and she never had no good times
after the war

at school they keep telling us
another war is about ready
and i ready too
to get some of them good times

Thomas Holy-Flute

The coyote in the water reeds
catching crayfish for his dinner
can no longer catch the rabbit,
the snake, the squirrel, the gopher.

A green and yellow sickness
is closing down his eyes,
sewing up his pocket-ears,
stopping up his nose.

His fur is torn and sparse
and hanging on his bones;
his legs are minus one, his nails
worn down to none.

And oh his teeth! his prideful teeth
like mine no longer latch;
so side by side we wait to eat
whatever each may catch.

John Knew-The-Crow 1880

I saw a blue-winged bird
sitting silent in the marsh,
his brothers flown away.
Ice grew among his feathers.

I saw a snake
in the forest rock.
She gave me warning, I gave her none;
I wear hers against my breast.

I saw the buffalo in rut.
They could not see me
for the earth ran away into the sky,
and the sound carried off the sun.

I saw the turtle on the grass,
too big, too blind to move.
His neck died beneath my ax,
but the claws walked on toward the water.

I saw my mother and my father die,
and the soldiers took me away.

Emmet Kills-Warrior
Turtle Mountain Reservation

1
nobody know what i got inside
but i think to tell it all
how it is to be indian
on the reservation
where i was born
where i grow up
where i die

2
i live in a government house
eat government food
go to their school
where i read about black people
live in a crowd in a city
see pictures where they all mad
at rats in their houses

3
i would like to live in a city
i would like to get mad
at a thing like rats

4
they told me
we take care of your mama
in government hospital
she get their funeral too
my brother at their war
my sister in their jail
i come out to the prairie
sit on old rock
i think about old days
when the indian didnt have
no government
to be born or die

5
well that what i got inside
that my story
the government can go shit

Seth Dismounts Thrice Rapid City, So. Dak., 1967

1
seth dismounts thrice
caught josephine
his new wife
in somebodys bed
took his thirty-thirty carbine
got in korea
shot them dead

2
seth had the idea
to go tell the police
but instead
went to the star-
light found denise
eagle-ear at the bar
and then she said
did he want a piece
drunk he did it drunk
in halley park
but her head broke
it went thunk
on a rock in the dark

3
seth thinks it good joke
for some fat white
lady tourist to find
in daylight
but three times bad sign
for dumb indian buck
next day police find him
seth say it just his luck

4
i say it sure been
one fucked up
high price night
for seth dismounts thrice

Charlie Two-Head
White Shield, No. Dak., 1968

1
my sister betty
got charlie last winter
we all like him
when he new
one day we go to town
charlie stayed to home
we all come back
betty look at him then
he got blood
coming out the nose
out the eyes
lots of flies
all around
we wash him up
he dont move any
betty dont want police
to ask questions
at night she put him
in lake

2
it get summer again
the ice go away
people with big boats
come fishing
a white man catch charlie
thought he got big catfish
haul him in
has heart attack
i hear about it

3
and i think
charlie full of surpise
like when betty get him

and when we find him dead
and when he got fished out
from the lake

Bessie Dreaming Bear
Rosebud, So. Dak., 1960

we all went to town one day
went to a store
bought you new shoes
red   high heels

aint seen you since

Lila Good-Weasel
Standing Rock, No. Dak.

my grandma lives
on porcupine creek
it only about

this   wide

since it dried
up six years past
when grandpa died
of the flu

she got one room
one bed and one blanket
she dont need no more

she got white eyes
from cataracts
the doctor say
and water in her legs
and belly
they like to swell up
like to bust

she lose a lot
every night
peeing in her bed
and crying all day

so much water in her
it just leaks out
all the time
and i think the creek
would get

THIS   WIDE

pretty soon
maybe she will drown first

Thomas Iron-Eyes
Born *circa* 1840.
Died 1919, Rosebud Agency, S.D.

1

I woke before the day, when the night bird
Knocked three times upon my door
To warn the Other Sleep was coming.
By candlelight I painted the two broad stripes
Of white across my forehead, the three scarlet spots
Upon my cheek. I greased well my braids
With sour fat from the cooking pot, then tied them
With a bit of bright string saved for the occasion.
From the trunk I took the dress of ceremony,
The breechclout and the elkskin shirt,
The smoke of their breaths strong in my nose;
Smoke not of this time, this life or place,
But of my youth, of the many lodges I dwelt within;
The pony raids, the counting coup;
The smell of grass when it first was green,
And the smell of coming snows, when food was plentiful
Within the camp, and ice crept over the rivers.
Carefully I put on the dress, then the leggings with scalps,
As thin now and as colorless as the hair
Of sickly animals, sinew-tied along the seams;
And on my feet the red-beaded moccasins
Worn by none but the bravest of warriors.
I lie here, waiting, my dry bones and ancient skin
Holding my old heart.
The daystar finds me ready for my journey.

2

Another time, another life, another place,
My people would have wrapped me in deerskin,
Sewed me in the finest of furs;
then borne me in honor to the cottonwood bier,
Laying at my right hand the sacred pipe,
And at my left the arrows and bow, the lance
I long ago bound with thongs and hung
With the feathers from the eagle's breast.
Below the scaffold of the dead

My pony of the speckled skin and fierce heart
Would be led, and with a blow of the stone ax
Upon his skull, lie down to wait my need.
I would know that far above
In the sacred hoop of the sky
Long-sighted hawks, hanging on silent wings,
Marked my passage.

3

When the Life-Giver hid from the night,
The dark wind would speak to my spirit
And I would arise, taking up my weapons.
Mounting my horse I would follow
The great path over the earth,
The road leading to the Old Grandfathers
Beyond the stars.
I would see the glow of their cooking fires
Bright as arrow tips across the northern sky;
Waiting for me, old friends dance and feast
And play the games of gambling.
Behind me drums would beat, and willow whistles cry
Like the doves of spring who nested
In the berry bushes near the river by my village.
I would pause to hear my sons in council
Speaking of my deeds in war, my strength and wisdom,
Praising me; knowing my women in their sorrow
Were tearing their clothing, their faces bloodied
And smeared with ashes.

4

But I am Thomas. I am here,
Where no grass grows, no clear rivers run;
Where dirt and despair abound,
Where heat and rain alike rust out
The souls of my people, the roofs of tin;
Where hunger sits in the dooryards,
Where disease, like a serpent, slips from house to house.
I am Thomas, waiting for the wagon
To bring the government box of pine;
Waiting for the journey to the burying ground
Below sandy buttes where rattlesnakes
Stink in burrows, and the white man's wooden trinities
Stand in crooked rows.

There I shall be put beneath the earth.
There shall my spirit be sealed within
The planks of the coffin.
There I shall not hear the dark wind's cry
To come and ride the starry road
Across the holy circle of the sky.

Last Summer It So Happened

Last summer my neighbor
refused a future
whose base materials were
a heart of fat,
a lean purse,
and an unending thirst.

In the forty-fifth year
of his life
by starlight he placed
the barrel of a rifle
into his mouth
and ate of its silver fruit.

But a bit of his head
flew over my fence
and fell in my garden.
Picking flowers the following day,
I thought it a toadstool,
until I leaned down and touched.

This summer my garden grew
nothing but weeds:
I fear my neighbor sowed
random seeds.
I fear for my head.
I fear the future.

Why I Chose to Live in the Desert

One morning a Voice spoke to me.   It said,
My son: Choose what of this world
you want for your own,
and I considered an ocean or a prairie,
but settled for a mountain.
That same day I went to the County Courthouse
with the title in my hand;
a deed in perpetuity
with stamps and seals and an Indisputable Signature,
and it was recorded I owned a mountain.

I took good care of my mountain,
fencing it well, hiring men with guns
and silent faces to tend my boundaries,
while I kept vigilant watch,
protecting my possession.

But lightning set fire to the forests,
and animals fouled the paths;
snakes and lizards ripened in the rocks,
and the fences were stricken with blight.
The men with guns fell to feuding
and died of their wounds or moved on.
It made me realize owning a mountain
had been a bad choice and I moved to the desert.
Here, all Voices are lost on the wind.

The Journey

These horses eat from pails,
dew beading the rims
like silver bracelets gleaming
in the morning sun.

These horses bend their necks
to receive the harness,
soft as a summer's afternoon
against their sable skins.

These horses hide their eyes
beneath plumes of darkness
and walk on ivory feet,
taking the familiar path.

I the driver,
I the passenger.

Spirit Lake, Minnesota

the summer storm comes over the lake
from out of the west
red thunder cracks the sun
and drives before it
great flocks of sheep
the little lambs drowning
in the purple foam

then the wind goes to sleep
in the tall grasses
of summer's twilight
and i hear water birds mourning
their lost children
whose small green feathers
unfold on the gentle waves

June the Twenty-Second

Down in the thickets
the locusts are sewing
their shrouds as the spiders
spin snares of lace;
and deep in the shadows,
lunching on lizards,
lies the goldenskinned buttontailed snake.

And in and beyond them,
under and over the grass and the dirt,
sober and somber, blundering blindly,
ants dig their tunnels
diverse in the earth;
hasty and rude, desperate for food
to nourish their seasonal race.

While out in the meadow
atop the blue clover
a dragonfly chooses her lover.

New Year's Eve

i wanted to go home but things kept breaking down
and my money kept getting older
and time kept caving in like sand
until the day before the new year

then my house fell apart late in the afternoon
and it was time for a drink so i went to the market
and they were celebrating new years eve
in the central square of some city

i liked the torches and costumes
and the music (but not quite)
then a man said to me where is your body
i wasnt sure of an answer

i said id watch a while before i told
well you need a body you know he said
and i said well you see it right here
and he shouted you cant crucify yourself

so i looked about and everybody had a body
besides his own and there were crosses in the square
and every so often they nailed up a body
it seemed quite orderly and and reasonable

he said go buy a body
at the store next to the church
theyre cheap and a bargain tonight
i thanked him for his advice

the lady at the counter was most helpful
but all she had left were children
you should have come earlier she said
by now every body is well picked over

i counted the money so old in my purse
just enough for a bottle or body
it wasnt hard to make a choice
given the circumstances

so i bought a girl of nine or ten
with a handful of nails thrown in
and i pegged that kid to a cross as fast
as id toss off a glass of gin

and everyone cheered and applauded
while i carried a torch round the square
i liked the torches and costumes
and the music (even less than before)

i never got home because of the things that broke
i never got home because my money got old
i never got home because the months had holes
nothing got better

Fishing on Lake Metigoshe

bluebottles wheel
between me and the arabs
billowing through
the blue desert that is
the sky

the sun breathes yellow
my hook brings up
an empty clamshell
from the bottom of the glass

we laugh at one another
he wider
and better
while the white butterfly
who rests on the oar
claps his wings
in silent applause

It Was The Season

it was the season of locusts
and the day was so hot
my hair melted
it ran down my back like wax

it was the season of hornets
and the day was so hot
my eyes fused
they ran down my face like lava

it was the season of beetles
and the day was so hot
my head blew up and the sun went out

The Red Fox

A winter day on the prairie
finds me in a bus
going nowhere
through a nowhere
of grey snow
and the bus grey also
only the road ahead
real enough
to lead somewhere

It is cold
prairie cold
and the prairie runs grey
up hills not there
runs over the bus and down
crossing the dark windrow
following us

My breath is a wet
circle of existence
against the window
through which I glimpse
the fox
sitting in his singular sunset
the wind sleeking his fur

Poets/Poems

I am the chariot
rolling through alleys
on philosophic wheels.
Follow me and be blinded
in my fiery dust.

I am the bird
moulten with love,
wingless in the thicket.
Bend close and be bitten
by the snake beside me.

I am the box
within a box
within a box.
Open me and be deafened
by my shadow.

I am the unicorn
feeding in the forest
on leaves of glass.
Stalk me and be wounded
by a flowering arrow.

I am the eye
without a lid
looking at you.

Poets/Poems

i cast in ever wider circles
while the wind tricks my senses
and the clouds
roll across the earth
like shadow rocks,
my shadow racing before them

infinite is this field
a remote and secret place
where i hunt

language nests in this field
i am the seeker
come to steal its fledglings

words

Poets/Poems

Mainly,
the truthful man
makes a wretched poet;
honesties are necessary
for those of good character.

However,
lies are lean wisdoms,
lies are our moral climates;
they leave the taste of music
in our mouths.

Thus,
this is a poem,
a piece of glass
we look at each other through.

Dacotah Winter

It is this:
it is where all compass points
show north

where the days are cancelled out
by a sluggish moon
and the wheel of the sun
is broken

it is where wolves wait
in white caves
sniffing pale winds
red mouths watching

it is where the long-fingered
hand of winter
clangs down a crystal lid
to the sound of snow

it is where the doe-eyed mouse
in her green gold nest
sleeps.

A Successful Retirement

I was born, was married at thirty, retired at sixty,
And could not admit I had no future.
So I spent my days making birdhouses, beer,
And a picket fence around the backyard.

But the birds refused my shelters, and the beer
Blew up. The fence fell apart during a high wind.
So I spent my time making a bomb in the cellar,
And it has taken months of labor and planning.

My wife would open the door, holler down,
"What are you doing down there?"
"Building a bomb," I'd say, and she'd go "Haha."
And tell the neighbors who came to morning coffee.

Then they would holler down, "Good luck with your bomb!"
But I kept working, getting the bomb finished, thinking,
"To hell with birds, to hell with beer, to hell with fences."
My bomb was beautiful, proof of personal success.

One day at breakfast my son Joe asked, "How's the bomb?"
And I said "DONE! by God." But he just said, "Gimme
Twenty till payday," and Millie talked about her acne,
My wife about her dentist, took out her uppers to show me.

I told myself: They are all just failure-examples,
Like my birdhouses, my beer, and my picket fence.
Tonight I intend to demonstrate my bomb-achievement,
And we shall all retire.

To Billie Jean: Streetwalker
Who At One Time Was A Rockette

She stands beneath the light
waiting for the cue
and when the horns signal
she lifts her head
smiling she waves
her broken arms then
begins her dance
on legs corroded
with veins of old cruelties
dances alone in the night
her final appearance

Marnie Walsh is a native Dakotan who received her B.A. degree from Pennsylvania State University and her M.A. in Creative Writing from the University of New Mexico (Albuquerque). In 1973, while completing her Master's, she received a National Endowment for the Arts Fellowship. Although she has traveled in Europe and Mexico, she prefers the Dakotas where she lives in a remote canyon in the Black Hills. Presently she is at work on her third novel.

Ms. Walsh's poetry from **A Taste of the Knife** has been selected for inclusion in the Pushcart Press **Best of the Small Presses** anthology.

Ahsahta Press

POETRY OF THE WEST

MODERN-

Norman Macleod, *Selected Poems*
Gwendolen Haste, *Selected Poems*
Peggy Pond Church, *New & Selected Poems*
Haniel Long, *My Seasons*
H. L. Davis, *Selected Poems*
Hildegarde Flanner, *The Hearkening Eye*
Genevieve Taggard, *To the Natural World*
Hazel Hall, *Selected Poems*
Women Poets of the West: An Anthology

CONTEMPORARY-

Marnie Walsh, *A Taste of the Knife*
Robert Krieger, *Headlands, Rising*
Richard Blessing, *Winter Constellations*
Carolyne Wright, *Stealing the Children*
Charley John Greasybear, *Songs*
Conger Beasley, Jr., *Over DeSoto's Bones*
Susan Strayer Deal, *No Moving Parts*
Gretel Ehrlich, *To Touch the Water*
Leo Romero, *Agua Negra*
David Baker, *Laws of the Land*
Richard Speakes, *Hannah's Travel*

BOISE STATE UNIVERSITY
BOISE, IDAHO 83725